Mi(

MW01289205

WINSTON CHURCHILL:
LEADERSHIP LESSONS
The great teachings of the last lion

© 2... by Michael Winicott.

... by UNITEXTO

Published by UNITEXTO

Table of Contents

Introduction

Great leaders are never born that way. They create themselves through hard work and determination, a lifelong process of learning, self-assessment, and struggle. Through this toil, truly effective leaders build up the inner strength and self-possession that allow them to inspire and motivate others to do greater things, mirroring through other people the way they maximize their own potential.

Winston Churchill is one of the most fascinating figures of the recent past, for a wide variety of reasons. One of the most compelling of these is how his life so definitively embodies this process of becoming a great leader. Churchill fought to make the most of himself and of others around him almost from the start, and the times and setting he lived in gave him no shortage of challenges to test himself against.

This short book aims at helping those interested in the subject of leadership appreciate a few of the many lessons that Churchill's life has to offer. It begins with a brief overview of the great man's life story, ranging from the aristocratic, but often challenging, circumstances of his birth and early life to the height of his power and his subsequent decline.

It then moves onto ten especially significant lessons in leadership from that famous life, each springing from the circumstances of a particular stage of his development and his responses to them. While each of these distinct episodes has a particular point to teach to students of leadership, they also help to reveal and illuminate more fundamental principles that are just as valuable.

Churchill's life has far more to teach than could possibly be covered in a short work like this, so what follows should not be taken as anything more than a taste of what is available. Even a relatively quick and casual survey of what the man's life and experiences can offer should be valuable, though, to those interested in becoming stronger, more effective leaders themselves.

Winston Churchill's Life in Brief

Winston Leonard Spencer-Churchill was born, nearly two months prematurely, on November 30, 1874, at Blenheim Palace in England. Churchill's aristocratic father and American-born mother were distant, putting him largely in the care of a nanny of whom he would say after her death that "she was my favourite friend."

Churchill was willful and rebellious from an early age, demonstrating unmistakable intelligence but performing poorly at each of a succession of schools he attended. At the age of 14, he scored so highly on the placement examination for the Harrow School, on the outskirts of London, that he was enrolled in the most demanding math classes the institution had to offer. Soon thereafter he impressed his teachers with a similar aptitude for history, but continued producing the same dismal grades, thanks to his rebelliousness.

Unable or unwilling to graduate from the Harrow School, Churchill enrolled in the Royal Military College with the aim of starting upon a military career that would eventually allow him to follow in his soon-to-be departed father's footsteps as a politician. Buckling down under the more disciplined environment he found himself in, he graduated eighth in his class, accepting a commission as a second lieutenant cavalry officer.

While in the military and as a war correspondent for a number of London-based newspapers, the young Churchill traveled widely, spending time in Cuba, India, Sudan, and South Africa over the course of the next decade. He made time during this period to win his first position in government as a Member of Parliament in the House of Commons, eventually being appointed First Lord of the Admiralty in 1911, before resigning in 1915 to fight on the Western Front in what would come to be known as the Great War.

After the war, Churchill resumed his political life, rising to become Chancellor of the Exchequer under a Conservative Party government, before watching his fortunes quickly dwindle after a string of setbacks in short succession. With his reputation at large having already suffered greatly, he damaged his standing with the Conservative Party further through another pair of incidents, leaving many to wonder if his ascent through the world of politics might have come to an end.

During this trying time, Churchill occupied himself largely with writing and his duties in the House of Commons, becoming known for his warnings about the threat posed by a militarily ambitious Germany. Though he failed to provoke the British military buildup that he prescribed, his political record, military experience, and basic acceptability to many across the political spectrum led to his selection as

Prime Minister in a coalition government not long after the United Kingdom declared war on Germany.

Churchill quickly distinguished himself through his ability to inspire the citizens and troops of the United Kingdom, delivering, in short order, several of his most famous speeches soon after taking office. Convincing the public that, however difficult the task and long the odds, the Fascist powers had to be resisted, Churchill was also highly successful at rallying the international support and coordination that would eventually help win the war.

Summarily upon the war ending, he was turned out of office. He remained active in politics as a Member of Parliament for the next six years, however, biding his time and warning against the dangers posed by the nakedly ambitious Soviet Union, as with the famous "Iron Curtain" speech he gave in Missouri. He took up the post of Prime Minister once again in 1951, fighting to preserve the remaining British Empire and cultivating the relationship with the United States that he had worked so hard during the war at building up.

After suffering a series of strokes, he stepped down as Prime Minister in 1955, at the age of 80, eventually giving up his seat in the House of Commons in 1964. A final stroke felled him in 1965, when he was 90 years old. The funeral that followed was the largest in world history up until that time, with every nation on earth save China sending representatives, and over 300 million people watching on television.

10 Lessons in Leadership from Winston Churchill

1: Turn Weakness into Strength

The young Winston Churchill was in several ways an unlikely candidate for greatness. With no particular physical gifts, displaying little in the ways of robustness or athleticism, he was similarly lacking in the obvious courage that would eventually come to define him in the eyes of many.

Another of his deficits was a pronounced speech impediment, a difficulty forming 's' sounds that is today known as a lateral lisp. One expert at the time told Churchill that his tongue was inhibited "by a ligament which nobody else has," although another doctor, Sir Felix Semon, advised Churchill in 1897 that nothing in the way of natural potential held back his speaking, and that he only needed to concentrate diligently on honing his speaking skills.

As he would throughout his later life, Churchill chose to keep his head down and focus on improvement, rather than giving in to what some might have considered the inevitable. He spent long hours practicing words and phrases that were heavy with 's' sounds, working to overcome a problem that had at first been so pronounced that few had failed to notice it.

Over the years, that work paid off greatly, so that signs of this speech difficulty are often hard to discern in his recorded speeches today. Even having made great progress, Churchill kept at his exercises throughout his life, in addition to seeking out other avenues of relief, like the making later on of a special set of dentures designed to address the problem.

Thanks to this hard, unwavering work, then, there came a time when the demanding Churchill himself could say that his "impediment [was] no hindrance," with the young man who had sometimes struggled with basic communication gaining confidence and even fame as a public speaker. He would go on, in fact, to become one of the twentieth century's most highly regarded and influential orators of all, thanks far more to his hard work over the decades than to any natural gifts.

Although he came from a privileged background and had plenty of advantages, Churchill also fought ferociously throughout his life to become the leader he is known as today. His early and long-lasting struggles with his speech impediment not only gave him the ability to communicate with and inspire others more effectively, they helped to give him the discipline and perspective that set the stage for many other accomplishments.

Throughout his life, Churchill would remain an intensely studied public speaker, relying on preparation and practice of his speeches to an extent that few others of the time's greatest orators did. In focusing so intently on overcoming his lateral lisp, he had also paved the way for success of an even greater sort, giving himself the ability to look at his speech and oratory in an objective, detached way that paid great dividends throughout his career as a public figure.

While there can be no doubt that the greatest leaders invariably have many natural gifts, it is equally true that they also work harder than many suppose to overcome their deficits, often creating new strengths in the process. Churchill's struggle with his speech impediment is a fine example of this phenomenon, as a little boy with a marked difficulty went on to become one of the most admired speakers of the last hundred years and more.

For those setting out to maximize their own potential as leaders, then, it is important to remember that, as Churchill's example shows, even history's most accomplished leaders had to fight and struggle to achieve what they did. In fact, these sustained efforts, beyond shoring up weaknesses, often reveal or produce new strengths along the way, as well.

2: Leverage Every Tool at YourDisposal
In addition to working hard and consistently to overcome his weaknesses, Churchill was just as diligent about realizing the full potential of his many strengths. With an intense ambition to succeed in the

world of British politics like his father had, he chose a proven, traditional path into that realm by joining the military. Before long, however, he would add a far less common calling to his resume, one that would eventually prove to define him just as much as his inspiring oratory, unflinching courage, or titanic resolve.

As a young second lieutenant, Churchill received an annual stipend of £300, a substantial sum that was nonetheless insufficient to allow him to keep up with the lifestyles of the other aristocratic military officers. A supplement from his mother helped, but Churchill realized early on that he would need to find another source of income that would mesh well with his military obligations and political ambitions.

He soon found that in writing. Churchill had been a consistently poor student right up until finally excelling at the Royal Military College, but he had always displayed a keen intelligence and a startling perceptiveness. Early in his adult life, he began deploying these assets alongside his inimitable wit, becoming a popular war correspondent for several London newspapers, eventually graduating to writing books, and thereby becoming entirely self-sufficient in financial terms.

In time, Churchill would come to be recognized as one of the twentieth century's greatest writers, even to the point of winning the prestigious Nobel Prize in

Literature. His work as a war correspondent would further his political career in important ways, taking him to Cuba during that country's War of Independence and to South Africa as the Second Boer War raged, with both incidents raising his public profile greatly.

In addition to directly furthering his political ambitions and furnishing him with a comfortable livelihood, Churchill's writing would provide him with a productive outlet when the tides turned against him. He famously wrote two of his most important works, *Marlborough: His Life and Times* and *A History of the English Speaking Peoples*, during a period when many thought that his political career had come to an end, staying productive, positive, and focused at a time when many would have given in to feelings of defeat.

To excel at such a high level in a sphere completely separate from one's primary focus is certainly unusual, but it is the kind of thing that truly singular leaders regularly achieve. Those looking to make the most of their own leadership potential can learn from how Churchill refused to succumb to an overly narrow focus, recognizing and cultivating a strength in his writing ability that made him a fuller, more complete leader and human being. A leader who makes the most of every strength in this way will always have more resources to fall back on in difficult times and to leverage when the time is right for pushing ahead.

13

3: Bounce Back Quickly and Seek New Opportunities

Even more so than with the careers of most great political leaders, Churchill's was marked by ups and downs. His began, in fact, with a pair of adverse events that likely would have put a stop to the ambitions of most people of lesser will and perseverance. By refusing to be forestalled or feel defeated, Churchill emerged from this early period a much stronger person and one whose political potential had been greatly enhanced.

His initial defeat was a common electoral one, as he failed to win the seat he had contested in a special election in 1899. Having been thrust into the public consciousness through his exploits in Cuba, India, and the Sudan, as well as his extensive writings about the developments he saw, he seemed like a strong candidate for the incumbent Conservative Party to sponsor for the borough of Oldham. Churchill campaigned impressively, thereby catching the eye of many longtime political observers, but better organization on the part of the opposing Liberal Party saw him defeated.

Undeterred, Churchill, casting about for a new opportunity, accepted a commission from London's *Morning Post* to cover the Second Boer War in South Africa, where he was captured along with a contingent of British troops as they traveled by armored train.

14

Despite acting as a reporter and not being a member of the military at the time, Churchill distinguished himself greatly in the struggle, a fact that would become widely known in Britain before long.

After working with other prisoners of war to create maps that depicted troop movements and other facts of military interest, Churchill escaped the camp where he was held, covering 300 miles before finding safe harbor. Upon returning to England, he found himself a celebrity of sorts, a development that allowed him to easily cruise to victory in the 1900 general election, taking the seat that he had lost so ignominiously barely more than a year before.

Although he had lost that first election in a fairly disheartening way, Churchill had never for the moment given in to feelings of defeat or pessimism. He had eagerly sought out his next opportunity, realizing that he had to make the most of his time if he was to realize his potential, despite being only 25 years old at that point.

Even when another, seemingly crushing defeat in the form of his capture followed soon after, Churchill remained positive and open to opportunity, making the best of his time in the prison camp by creating valuable military maps. When the moment was right, he bravely struck out and escaped back to his native country to easily claim the prize that had so recently been denied him.

No leader of any significance, of course, can go entirely without experiencing defeat. Successfully dealing with such downturns and unwelcome developments, in fact, is often what distinguishes the greatest of leaders from those a rank below, and Churchill was one of the most impressive of all in this respect. These early experiences would be only a few of many that would ultimately impact his life and career, and one of the most striking things about him as a leader is how resolutely he always refused to accept defeat, often discovering new opportunities in doing so.

Those looking to apply the lessons of Churchill's experience to their own lives and leadership endeavors should commit themselves to seeking out new opportunities whenever existing ones have receded, whether temporarily or for good. Part of what gives a leader the ability to direct others productively is the ability to identify new prospects quickly and accurately, where others are left without direction.

4: Stand on Principle, Even When the Costs Seem High

Having finally found his way into Parliament, the young Churchill might have been expected to lay low. Soon after winning his seat, however, he found himself torn between the Conservative Party he belonged to and his own principles. Churchill was convinced that free trade between nations was the best way of

16

building prosperity for all, but the Conservatives were pushing a protective scheme of tariffs and other regulations designed to shield British businesses from foreign competition.

Refusing to toe the party line, Churchill gave a number of well-received speeches before Parliament expressing his point of view, much to the consternation of the more senior members of his party. Undeterred, Churchill continued to advocate for free trade against the wishes of party leaders, intransigence that soon saw him effectively shut out from Conservative deliberations and support. All the same, Churchill continued pushing for free trade in an evocative and persuasive way, producing memorable lines like "to think you can make a man richer by putting on a tax is like a man thinking that he can stand in a bucket and lift himself up by the handle."

Only a few years into his political career, then, Churchill switched sides, crossing over to join the opposing Liberals, a party of generally *laissez-faire* principles which had long rallied for the free trade measures he had supported so ably. This move gave him the freedom to continue pushing for his pet economic cause and soon produced even greater dividends when, in 1905, the Liberals were able to form a government, thereafter naming Churchill Under-Secretary of State for the Colonies, a position that would grant him particular influence over another area of special interest to him.

For such a young, wholly inexperienced Member of Parliament to switch parties so soon after being elected was not entirely unprecedented, but it was not regarded as boding well for the career that would follow. Churchill stood bravely by his principles throughout the period, giving the position advocated by his party due consideration, but refusing to be silenced when he found it wanting. What might have been taken as a sign of fickleness and lack of commitment in other leaders was instead recognized and rewarded, in Churchill's case, as a stand made on the basis of genuine principle and producing therefore new opportunities for the young legislator.

Although Churchill would remain within the Liberal Party for a number of years, finding that he had some real affinity with its platform, he would eventually decide once again that the Conservatives were a better fit for his temperament and worldview. After dabbling for a few years as one of a few "Constitutionalists" who focused on opposing the growing spread of socialism, Churchill returned to the Conservative Party in 1924, pithily saying that "anyone can rat, but it takes a certain ingenuity to re-rat." Despite his having strayed from it so early and prominently, the Conservative Party would remain his political home for the rest of his life.

Because Churchill was so forthright and visibly independent, these moves that could have cost a lesser leader a career ultimately did nothing to harm his. A less courageous leader might have been inclined to prevaricate or censor himself as he came into conflict with his party, but Churchill's consistency and transparency ensured that he earned respect, instead of condemnation, for switching parties as he did. In fact, the way in which he crossed party lines again and again likely helped paved the way for his first selection as Prime Minister later on.

A true leader, then, must willingly and repeatedly grapple with difficult issues like this one, when principle and conviction have to be weighed against the costs that sticking to them might seem to impose. Only through this struggle can a leader develop a sense for what the best course of action is likely to be.

5: Innovate to Challenge Conventional Wisdom
During his first stint as Britain's First Lord of the Admiralty between 1911 and 1915, Churchill pushed hard to modernize the country's Navy, taking on entrenched interests ranging from the United Kingdom's coal producers to powerful military naysayers. Despite being of a markedly conservative temperament himself, Churchill recognized that airplanes would play an increasingly central role in future wars and that substituting fuel oil for coal would allow the ships of the country's formidable

Navy to project British power even more effectively around the world.

He was also an early proponent of the armored tank, a military vehicle that would prove to be decisive in the wars that would follow in the coming decades. None of these positions were entirely popular or common ones at the time that Churchill began advocating in these directions, but they all eventually proved correct.

The most immediately significant of these projects was Churchill's order that future British battleships would be built with engines that ran on petroleum, instead of the coal-fired boilers that powered existing ones. This was a fairly radical decision, because Britain had substantial reserves of coal, but little ability at the time to produce much in the way of petroleum. Listening closely to the Navy's foremost experts, Churchill concluded that the advantages of oil as a fuel, including far greater thermal capacity and a greatly reduced logistical burden, would make up for this difficulty.

Supporting the plan required that the British secure supplies and strategic stockpiles of oil from abroad, which proved to be a major project in itself. Eventually, however, thanks to Churchill's prodding, the United Kingdom became a part owner of the Anglo-Persian Oil Company, operating in what is today called Iran, thereby establishing a strategic presence that would serve the country well in the decades to come.

As a result of Churchill's efforts and orders, the British Navy became even more powerful and nimble, capable of traveling further and refueling more quickly, while requiring less in the way of infrastructure and logistical support. Although the project had been difficult and had required marshaling all of his formidable energies, Churchill had succeeded in modernizing the Navy in ways that would pay dividends for many years.

A thoughtful person by nature, he had done so only after studying the issue extensively and taking in all of the best available advice. Once he had come to a conclusion on the matter, he had acted to ensure that every necessary detail would be taken care of, realizing that such a massive project could easily fail if every necessary piece were not attended to.

This conversion of the British Navy to oil power shows a less frequently remarked-upon side of Churchill as a leader, in that it was more a victory of administration and management than of inspiration or bravery. All the same, Churchill's consistent courage to stand behind what he had come to believe was right was a critical factor in the success of project, and something that those pursuing transformation and innovation in their own organizations can stand to learn from. Effective leaders seek out opportunities like these eagerly, learning everything they can about the possibilities, and then throwing the full weight of their capabilities behind the effort once the correct course has become clear.

6: Regroup and Gain New Perspectives

Having rejoined the Conservative Party in 1924 after a decade spent with the Liberals, Churchill was made Chancellor of the Exchequer, a position that lifted him to new heights of power. Once again, he acted boldly, pushing to return the United Kingdom to the gold standard, a move that was at odds with much of the advice from the world's leading economists that he had previously sought and considered.

Churchill would later identify this program as the single greatest mistake of his career, but he pushed it through as ably as he could once he had decided on the course of action. The resulting tightening of Britain's money supply put a harsh crimp on the country's economy, earning Churchill and other proponents criticism as industries and citizens began to flounder.

Alongside a worldwide economic downturn, this was more than enough to force the Conservative Party out of power in 1929, with Churchill receiving a special share of blame for having pushed so hard for the gold standard. Nearly disgraced, he left the Cabinet with a heavy burden on his shoulders, but soon rebounded into productive work once again.

With relatively little in the way of political opportunity before him, he focused more intently on his writing than ever before, producing some of his greatest works and refining and enshrining in words his political philosophy. From his outsider's vantage point, the ever-engaged Churchill also began warning about the dangers of German rearmament, a service that would be acknowledged before long. Even while the Fascist movements of continental Europe initially seemed determined to combat the forces of communism and socialism, Churchill also remained on guard against Fascism.

Although much of it took place entirely off the stage of politics, Churchill's activity during this period was to prove every bit as consequential as the rest of his career. During these "wilderness years," as he called them, he remained every bit as attentive to his passions and goals as ever before, whether in the form of seeking to guide Britain to safety and prosperity or through supporting his family with his writing. Years later, when he would be named Prime Minister for the first time or receive the Nobel Prize in Literature, it was this period of virtual exile that laid the groundwork.

No leader can always remain at the forefront of things, so the greatest learn is to make the most of those times when circumstances shuffle them into the background. Churchill's intensely cultivated resilience and focus allowed him to push through what could have been a demoralizing period in productive, rewarding ways, adding new layers of capability to his arsenals. Others who wish to make the most of their own potential as leaders can learn greatly from this by refusing to allow setbacks, however great, to keep them from developing further.

7: Hold Steady Against Impossible Odds

With memories of the brutality and senselessness of the First World War still fresh in the minds of many, the British people were not inclined to confront an increasingly belligerent Germany only a couple of decades later. Although he would eventually be accused of overstating his influence in this respect, Churchill was undoubtedly one of the most prominent of those who tried to alert the country to the dangers that Germany presented, even while the country's acting leaders pursued an ultimately futile policy of appeasement.

Understanding how easy it would be to fall prey to charges of hysteria by those who wished to prevent a confrontation with Germany, Churchill sought to remain calm and consistent in his messaging, while still trying with all his might to make the point that Britain could not afford to give in to Teutonic demands. One of the most prominent voices of this sort in the House of Commons throughout the escalating tensions of the 1930s, he was attacked consistently by both the press and other politicians, but he remained firm.

Ultimately Churchill was unable to change the country's course from his position of relative powerlessness, with Britain's cheerful acceptance to Chamberlain's initially popular Munich Agreement with Hitler, a pact that would quickly prove the destructiveness of appeasement. As Chamberlain was feted as a hero by the British public, Churchill remained resolutely in opposition, garnering mostly scorn as a result.

Even with public opinion arrayed against him and his political stature at an all-time low, then, Churchill continued to make a case that no one wanted to hear. It could be taken as a failure of leadership that he failed to provoke the necessary action before Germany could storm over Europe, but the truth is that he was fighting insurmountable odds.

In the face of those odds, he and a few others did their absolute best to shake the country out of a deadly complacency and unwillingness to hear harsh truths. Challenges of this sort are among the greatest that leaders of any kind can face, as even the most principled can find their conviction and energies fading away in the face of such indifferent inertia and outright opposition.

Eventually, Churchill would earn the respect that he deserved for fighting so hard and so long to make his case, but only as Britain was plunged into a war that it could no longer avoid by any means, while having failed to build up her military as Churchill had advised. Although he had, in this respect, failed, Churchill had done everything that he possibly could to succeed and had refused to be cowed or dissuaded.

Those seeking to make the most of their own potential as leaders must recognize that there will be times that they, too, will face this kind of resistance and apathy, when their absolute best efforts fail to provoke the changes that are called for. Churchill's conduct throughout this period, then, has a lot to teach today's leaders about how to persevere and remain undefeated in such impossible situations.

8: Inspire Others to Do and Give More

If Churchill's efforts at persuasion had fallen on impossibly deaf ears throughout the 1930s, he would soon have a chance to use his talents to far greater effect. Many of his greatest challenges up until this point had been of a generally personal sort, with success requiring him to draw the best from himself, but he would now need to do the same for an entire nation.

As the German *Wehrmacht* rolled through Poland with an ease that few would previously have thought possible, and Britain finally declared war, Churchill

26

was restored to his previous position as First Lord of the Admiralty. It soon became clear that the architect of the failed policy of appeasement, Neville Chamberlain, was not equipped to lead the country in wartime, and had to resign. With no other obvious candidate for the country's highest political position, George VII tapped Churchill to lead the country as the Prime Minister of a coalition government, delivering him to his greatest goal at one of the most trying times in the nation's history.

Churchill wasted no time rallying the country behind him. He recognized from that start that Britain faced long odds, particularly as his exhortations about the need for a military buildup to match Germany's had been ignored throughout the 1930s. He saw that the desire to avoid the suffering that war would entail would be a powerful one, and immediately set out to inspire the British people to resist it, knowing that the price of succumbing would be too high.

He did so by cutting to the chase, laying out in clear, unflinching ways the difficult prospects that faced the country as it sought to hold out against Germany. At the same time, he inspired hope and courage in his nation's people by appealing to their pride and their love of their country and one another, crafting some of the most memorable images and speeches of his career during this period.

A lesser, less-confident leader might have sought to conceal the challenges that lay ahead, believing that only by doing so could the necessary support be rallied. In refusing to go this route, Churchill secured a confidence and loyalty from the British populace that would hold up through the ravages and pain of the war that followed, when so many would suffer and lose loved ones or their own lives.

Although he is probably best known as an orator, a leader for his wit and striking, inspiring imagery, Churchill ultimately owed just as much of his success to his ability to use these to support a plain, unblinking view of the world, however harsh it might have been. By being honest with his countrymen that tough times were to come and inspiring them from the beginning to confront them fearlessly, he succeeded in ways that few other leaders could possibly have hoped to match.

Leaders seeking to inspire others to bear up under difficulties and produce all that they are capable of, should keep in mind that the truth, properly framed and delivered, can be the most powerful motivator of all. It can take more in the way of skill and determination to lead in this fashion, but the results can be more reliable and valuable than if less straight forward means are employed.

9: Forge Relationships with Other Leaders, Admired and Otherwise

Even from the beginning of the war, Churchill and others recognized that defeating Germany outright would be practically impossible for Britain alone. While the country's navy was one of the world's most powerful, the island nation's army was much less formidable, making it no match for the beefed-up German Wehrmacht.

Churchill knew, then, that the United Kingdom would need all the help it could get if it was even to hold out hope, and he did not waste time pursuing it. The United States was the unknown quantity, an essentially friendly nation that was nonetheless disposed to isolationism, especially after the experiences of the First World War.

Early after assuming the position of Prime Minister, Churchill went to work on Franklin D. Roosevelt, who was then in his second term as President. Respecting that Roosevelt had his own countrymen's wishes to deal with, Churchill sought much-needed help for Britain while also continuing to plan for holding out against Germany alone.

The close relationship that developed between the two was to prove pivotal to the course of the war and to modern history. At Churchill's prodding, Roosevelt first secured aid for Britain in the form of critical supplies and fuel that allowed the country to continue resisting to the utmost of its ability.

Later on, the historic Lend-Lease program would outfit the British with even more in the way of military hardware, upholding the country's fighting capacity as the destruction of the war grated on it. Throughout this period, Churchill remained in close touch with Roosevelt, the deepening relationship between the two helping to forge even more substantial bonds between their countries. By the time the United States entered the war on Britain's side after the Japanese bombing of Pearl Harbor, Churchill's relationship with Roosevelt could rightly have been said to have been a major reason why Britain was able to hold out as long as it did.

Though he despised communism and instinctively distrusted Stalin, Churchill was also able to work with the Soviet leader in productive ways that redounded to Britain's benefit. Even while being leery about the threat the communist nation could pose once the war had concluded, Churchill recognized that dealing with Stalin was critical to bringing the conflict to an end as soon as possible.

Towards that end, he met personally with the communist leader a number of times, even going so far as to fly into Moscow in August of 1942. Although an undeniable and justified mutual distrust prevailed, these visits led to enough of a thaw between the two powerful men that they were able to coordinate their efforts against the Germans in ways that undoubtedly hastened the conclusion of the war and saved countless lives.

Through one man for whom he had genuine feelings of warmth and another for whom he did not, Churchill had found two critical allies for his stricken, desperate country. It can be tempting for those who take up the challenges of leadership to come to feel that they must, above all else, become self-sufficient, but it is also often the case that the most effective leaders seek and find help from others of the same rank when the moment is right. Learning how to work effectively and productively with other leaders, can prove to be every bit as important as the task of leading itself.

10: Living a Passionate, Well-Rounded Life

In addition to being complex, courageous, and resilient, Churchill was a thoroughly complete person. Some people who are as driven as he was come to seem one-dimensional, devoting the vast majority of their energies to a single calling. Churchill, on the other hand, never lost sight of the depth and variety of life's pleasures and opportunities, and he always set aside time, throughout his life, to recuperate and recharge himself, as well as experience new things, keeping his horizons fresh and stimulating.

In middle age, for example, Churchill was introduced to the art of oil painting, a pastime that he would involve himself until his death, even winning contests and selling some of his output under the pseudonym of "Charles Morin." He poured himself into painting like anything else he did, striving to do his best with every stroke of the brush, but used it to restore his energies for other pursuits, laughing off the suggestion that he was a serious artist.

Gardening had the same effect on him, and he retreated often throughout his life to the grounds of Chartwell, the estate he had purchased with the proceeds of some of his early writing work. Over the course of decades, despite the business and bustle of his life as a leader, Churchill and his wife Clementine transformed Chartwell into something even more beloved to them, shaping the grounds through their own hard work and plans. Churchill famously said that "a day away from Chartwell is a day wasted," a bit of exaggeration that aptly emphasized the truth of the estate's importance and centrality to his life.

Of course, Churchill is also famous for having been a passionate devotee of some of life's humbler pleasures, whether in the form of good whisky or great Cuban cigars. There are, of course, reasons to avoid such indulgences, but in Churchill's case they were simply the signs of someone who knew how to appreciate life in all of its fullness.

That depth of spirit and love of life, in fact, is undoubtedly a big part of what sets Churchill apart from so many other leaders of ostensibly similar stature. With a career that encompassed more in the way of turmoil, difficulty, defeat, and triumph than just about any other, Churchill seems larger than life in large part because he lived life so fully. For those leaders who become too narrowly focused, horizons can begin to shrink, such that a defeat or a setback can seem like the end of everything. For Churchill, there was always something else waiting around the corner, right up until the very end.

Conclusion

Fifty years after his death, Winston Churchill remains one of the most admired and popular leaders of all. His life story has a special attraction to those who themselves seek to lead others, because every twist and turn of it seems to offer a new and useful perspective on the undertaking.

A few common themes resonate throughout. First, whatever his considerable natural gifts, Churchill cultivated his leadership abilities consistently, throughout his entire life. From his early efforts to improve his speaking abilities or his attempts to jump-start his political career through military adventures, he was always challenging himself to do more and become more capable, even if this resolve rarely showed in his early academic performance.

Second, Churchill never succumbed to negativity or hopelessness, however desperate the situation seemed. Intimately familiar from an early age with what he called the "black dog" of depression, Churchill learned how to fight these attacks, pouring himself into activities, like writing, painting or gardening, that offered him distraction and relief. The resilience he built up in this way would eventually help him to inspire an entire nation through one of its darkest times, and likely gave him a depth of perspective that helped him to overcome difficulties that would have destroyed others. While most leaders will not share these experiences, the lesson of actively addressing negativity and hopelessness is an important and valuable one.

Third, Churchill would persevere where others would long since have given up. There is, of course, real danger in unthinking obstinacy, but Churchill's life more often illustrates the other side of the coin. Rather than bowing to the winds of popular sentiment or opposing viewpoints, he would explore the full implications of his convictions, struggling on even when he found himself alone. On occasion, he would find himself set back by his resolve, but he always made sure to learn something from the experience. Churchill's firmness of purpose was a way of taking the utmost from everything he did, allowing him to develop far more as a leader of people than those who are afraid or reluctant to commit themselves.

Finally, Churchill was the consummate individual, and he relished and prized his independence. Although he would go on to lead one of the greatest nations in the world, he ultimately answered to himself, with the discipline and hard work of his life allowing him to have final confidence in his judgments. Unmistakably flawed and sometimes even contradictory, Winston Churchill was humanity writ large in the form of one immensely inspiring and influential person.

Made in the USA
San Bernardino, CA
28 July 2017